SYMBOLS OF AMERICA

THE BALD EAGLE

KIM THOMPSON

NorwoodHouse Press

Cataloging-in-Publication Data

Names: Thompson, Kim.
Title: The bald eagle / Kim Thompson.
Description: Buffalo, NY : Norwood House Press, 2026. | Series: Symbols of America | Includes glossary and index.
Identifiers: ISBN 9781978575738 (pbk.) | ISBN 9781978575745 (library bound) | ISBN 9781978575752 (ebook)
Subjects: LCSH: Emblems, National--United States--Juvenile literature. | Bald eagle--United States--Juvenile literature. | Animals--Symbolic aspects--Juvenile literature. | United States--Seal--Juvenile literature.
Classification: LCC CD5610.T466 2026 | DDC 929.90973--dc23

Published in 2026 by
Norwood House Press
2544 Clinton Street
Buffalo, NY 14224

Designer: Rhea Magaro

Photo credits: Cover, p. 1 ArtesialD; p. 3 Katarzyna Hurova/Shutterstock.com; p. 4 Edwin Butter/Shutterstock.com; p. 5 Bryant Aardema/Shutterstock.com; p. 6 Steve Collender/Shutterstock.com; pp. 6, 8, 9 FloridaStock/Shutterstock.com; pp. 10, 12 Wikipedia; p. 11 photomaster/Shutterstock.com, p. 11 Library of Congress; p. 11 P&P/Shutterstock.com; pp. 13, 16 Library of Congress/Shutterstock.com; p. 15 A. Marino/Shutterstock.com; p. 17 Michele Ursi/Shutterstock.com; p. 18 YamabikaY/Shutterstock.com; p. 19 Regormark/Shutterstock.com; pp. 20, 21 NASA;

Printed in the United States of America

CPSIA compliance information: Batch #CSNHP26: For further information contact Norwood House Press at 1-800-237-9932.

THE BALD EAGLE

The bald eagle is a large bird of prey. White feathers on its head make it look “bald.” However, its name comes from the Old English word *balde*, which means “white.”

Bald eagles soar 10,000 feet (3,048 meters) high in the sky. Their wings can stretch eight feet (2.4 meters) wide. That's about the distance from the floor to the ceiling!

A SYMBOL OF AMERICA

The bald eagle is the official bird of the United States of America. It is a **symbol** of the country.

The U.S. is made up of 50 states. Each state has its own official bird. The bald eagle is different. It represents the entire nation.

The bald eagle **reflects** America. Both the bald eagle and the U.S. are found in North America. Both are big. Both are strong and powerful.

A flying bald eagle is **majestic**. It soars freely above Earth. It makes people think about being free. Having freedom is what many Americans **value** most.

Can you think of other ways that the bald eagle is like America?

HOW IT BEGAN

In the late 1700s, America was a new country. Leaders argued about what the national bird should be.

Benjamin Franklin was a leader from Pennsylvania. He said the bald eagle was “of bad moral character” like a robber. He said the turkey was “a much more respectable bird.”

In 1782, leaders in Congress voted for the bald eagle as the **emblem** for the new nation.

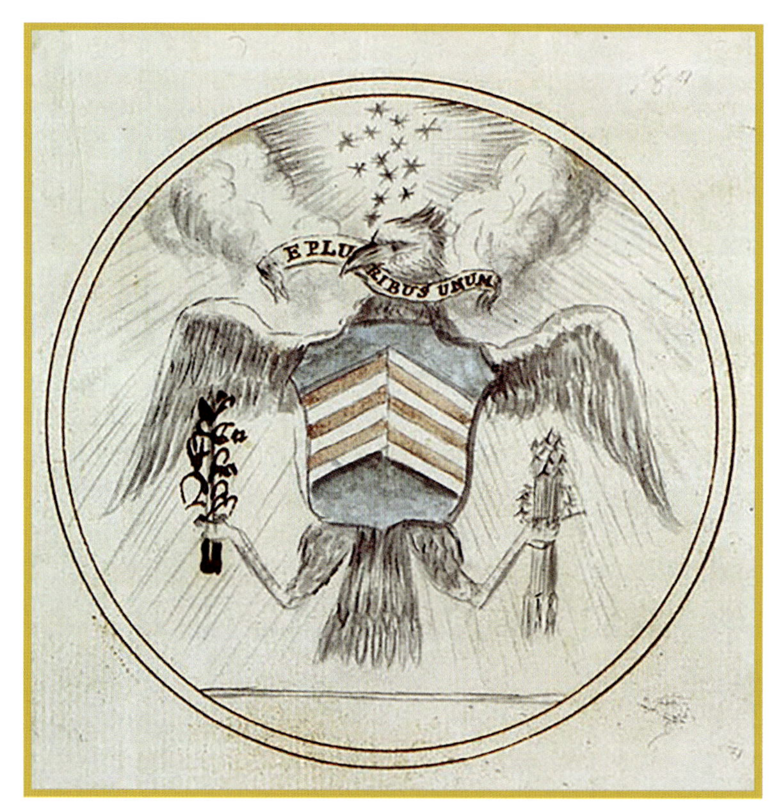

It was a good choice. In 1963, President John F. Kennedy wrote, “The **fierce** beauty and proud independence of this great bird aptly symbolizes the strength and freedom of America.”

SPOT THE SYMBOL

If you look closely, you will see the bald eagle on many things related to America.

It is on the Great **Seal** of the United States of America.

It is on the presidential flag.

It is on stamps.

A bald eagle tops the **mace** of the House of Representatives in Congress. This staff shows the right of leaders to make laws for the country.

Military **insignia** has bald eagles.

Bald eagles have been on U.S. **currency** ever since 1776. They are on today's quarters and dollar bills.

Special gold eagle coins were first made in 1986.

The bald eagle was the symbol of the astronauts who went to the moon in 1969. The lander was named the Eagle.

GLOSSARY

currency (KUR-uhn-see): money, including coins and paper bills

emblem (EM-bluhm): a symbol or sign that represents something

fierce (feers): strong, violent, or dangerous

insignia (in-SIG-nee-uh): badges, emblems, or designs that show someone's rank or membership in an organization, especially in the military

mace (mase): a rod or staff that is carried to show the power and authority of a government

majestic (muh-JES-tik): powerful and beautiful

reflects (ri-FLEKTS): shows or expresses

seal (seel): a design, stamp, or logo that is shown to make a document or other item official

symbol (SIM-buhl): an object or design that stands for, suggests, or represents something else

value (VAL-yoo): to believe that something is precious or important; to hold dear

THINKING QUESTIONS

1. What are the characteristics of a bald eagle?
2. How do the characteristics of a bald eagle relate to America?
3. What is a symbol? Why do you think countries have symbols?
4. What animal did Benjamin Franklin recommend as the national bird? Why?
5. Name three American objects that show bald eagles.

INDEX

ABOUT THE AUTHOR

Kim Thompson is a teacher and writer from Columbus, Ohio. She is an American history buff. She loves to travel to look at statues, monuments, and museums. She thinks it would be fun to do a scavenger hunt to search for symbols of the United States.